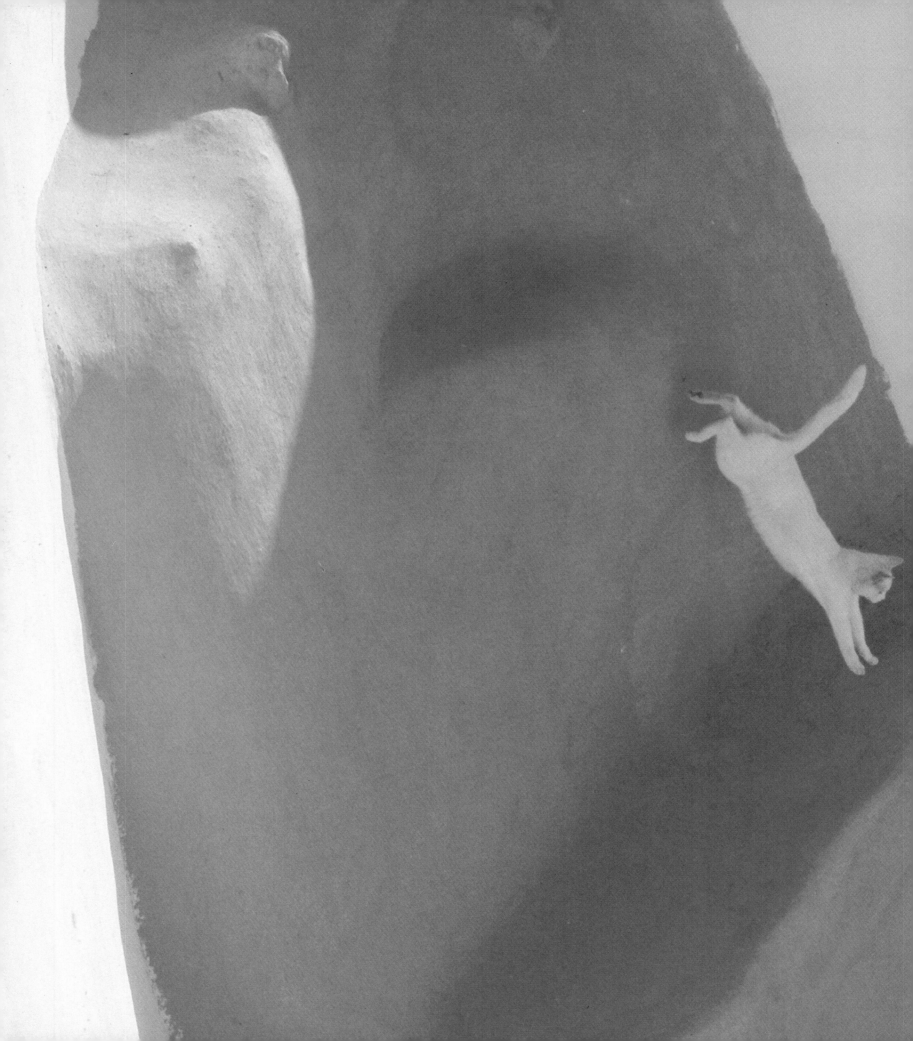

Hans Silvester

Sleeping
in the Sun

Carefree Cats of the Greek Islands

Thames and Hudson

Translated from the French SIESTE ET TENDRESSE
by Jane Brenton

First Published in Great Britain in 1997
by Thames and Hudson Ltd, London

Copyright © 1997 Éditions de La Martinière, Paris

British Library Cataloguing-in-Publication Data

A catalogue record for this book is available
from the British Library

ISBN 0-500-01822-7

Printed and bound in France

The Siesta

THE CATS YOU SEE ON THESE PAGES, slumbering peacefully, are masters of the art of relaxation.

The cats of the Greek islands can sleep anywhere – on a slab of concrete, on a carpet, or perched in a tree. They are, however, very particular about the place they choose for their siesta, whether in the sun or in the shade, on the ground or at some high vantage point, out in the open or snugly sheltered from the wind.

A cat may curl up in as many as ten different places in the course of a day, and every time his aim will be to achieve the greatest comfort consistent with safety. Even cats that are fast asleep don't allow themselves to be 'caught napping', but will start awake at the faintest of unfamiliar sounds.

To photograph sleeping cats, you must first win their absolute confidence. The slightest anxiety and they will shift position, no longer so totally relaxed. Another problem is that the Greek population is likely to be taking its siesta at the same time. The poor photographer is left in solitary contemplation of the snoozing cats, who are all the more easily disturbed by the one individual failing to observe the ritual siesta.

Over the years, I have followed my voyeuristic pursuits as discreetly as possible. In the Cyclades, as in any other part of the world, cats take a luxurious pleasure in the naps that are so essential to their well-being. To doze alone in an agreeable spot is a delight but, as you can see, to share a siesta with another, or with a group of others, compounds the enjoyment. And to be in love as well represents paradise on earth for any cat.

I love the institution of the siesta, unreservedly, and I often feel quite jealous as I watch these Greek cats. My greatest delight would be if these pictures were to inspire you to emulate them. To take a nap naturally, in the way they do, is not as easy as you might initially think. It requires a certain degree of practice and willpower. But if you can learn how to enjoy this form of carefree relaxation, then you will understand how, for a cat, the nap is the spice of life.

Sleeping at night is a necessity for which we are programmed by nature. Taking a siesta is something quite different. It is all to do with the pleasure of allowing yourself to settle down and doze and then finally drop off at leisure.

I am amazed, absolutely lost in admiration, when I see how these felines extract maximum enjoyment from their siesta – and this is as true of the meanest alley cat as it is of tigers, lions and leopards. From their claws to the tips of their tails, their whole bodies are devoted to relaxation, rest and pleasure.

Man's relationship with domestic animals has changed beyond recognition in the course of the last thirty years. Only two species, dogs and cats, have been lucky enough to be granted the status of man's best friend.

In developed countries, almost one in five of the population owns a cat or a dog. At first sight, this looks like outright luxury. The number of working dogs is tiny, and cats required to earn their keep as mousers are few and far between. Yet the money spent annually on these animals corresponds to the annual budget of some Third World countries. The fact is that these millions of cats and dogs play an important role in modern society. They give men, women and children a sense of contentment. Without them, life would be impoverished, the omnipresence of machines an ever more oppressive reality. Man has found a way to miniaturize certain breeds of dog so that some are no bigger than a cat – pets custom-made for the flat-dweller. Have you noticed how well they have adapted to our way of life? Dogs love car journeys and cats have learned to cope with our frequent changes of scene.

Their diet, too, has changed. It is no longer a matter of leftovers or titbits supplied by the butcher; instead, we now have specially prepared foods manufactured in ultra-modern factories.

Our four-legged friends are always ready to share their master's sorrows as well as his joys. For many of us, pets are our only defence against loneliness. Anyone who shares his life with an animal will appreciate that his companion views time in a completely different light. For the average tom, time is as free and boundless as air. He has no concept of the passing of years. His circumstances have improved beyond all recognition: he has plenty to eat, lots of affection, comfort and good medical care, and life rolls by pretty much without a worry. Only such phenomena as the motorized Parisian pooper-scooper reflect the problem posed by the increasing number of dogs living in towns.

Yet paradoxically the life of other domestic animals has considerably worsened. With the exception of the horse, whose dwindling numbers have assured its privileged position, other animals have been subject to modification by man, forced to become economically viable. Dairy cows have become milk factories, yielding a minimum of twenty-five litres a day, nine to ten thousand litres (some two thousand gallons) a year. Tied up their whole life long in cowsheds, little more than machines, they exist only for what they produce. Grazing in the fields, keeping their horns, being put to the bull, protecting their calves … all that belongs to a former age. Yet which of us doesn't have a mental picture of cows lying in a meadow full of flowers, peacefully chewing the cud?

It is not hard to see that milk produced under these conditions will never have the same quality or taste as that from a cow put out to graze. The meat from these poor beasts, forced to feed on meal made from ground-up animal corpses and never moving from the spot, ends up on the butcher's slab alongside that of cows who have lived their days out at pasture. People who have always supported progress and modernization are beginning to see the serious consequences of such enormities as transforming herbivores into carnivores in the name of profitability. Mad cows are made by mad men….

Pigs are reared in pig factories, by the million. Before long, they will probably be cloned and therefore identical. If consumers could see how these poor creatures live and die, they would feel differently about the pork chop sitting on their plate.

Pigs reared on farms and allowed to roam freely love their siestas. They wallow ecstatically in the mire and fall asleep in the sun, caked with mud.

The space allotted to a battery hen today is no bigger than the size of this book. The birds are there either to lay eggs or to be fattened, and that in record time. Whether they are happy or miserable or suffering from stress doesn't come into the equation. Man has found a way of enabling them to endure this life, by plying them with pharmaceutical products. The breeders are not peasant farmers; they are industrialists working in agribusiness, without scruples, obsessed with calculations of productivity and profitability.

Many good cooks have come to appreciate the consequences of this state of affairs and choose to obtain their produce from farmers who continue to rear poultry, pigs, rabbits and the rest in their natural surroundings, for their own consumption.

These animals are the lucky ones. They can still feel the sun, the rain, the air: they have a varied diet, and enjoy contact with each other and with man. They can move and sleep at will. They are allowed all the time they need to reach maturity, and when the day comes for them to be slaughtered, at least they are coming to the end of a life that was worth living. The quality of their meat testifies to that.

Nor is the future of wild creatures any more assured. Because of man's activities, the list of endangered animals constantly grows longer. The situation is serious. We know that every day fifty or more species become extinct. That means we are standing by and watching as twenty thousand species are lost every year.

In the Provençal countryside where I have lived for thirty-five years, I have noticed a spectacular reduction in the numbers of butterflies and other insects. Some birds have practically disappeared and the commonest mammals have become rare. When you walk in the hills in Provence, it is exceptional now to see a wild animal.

The chemical industry, intensive agricultural methods, shooting and traffic are the four main factors responsible for this holocaust.

As these changes gather pace, affecting domestic as well as wild animals, so man lavishes increasing affection on his dog or cat. It is a phenomenon repeated the world over.

There are certain boundaries that exist in nature, as for example the line in Europe at which olive trees begin to appear. South of that line, people indulge in the siesta. It is a break that is savoured, a moment of respite, profoundly rooted in Mediterranean culture. Life comes to a halt during the hottest hours of the day and only really picks up again towards evening. True, the custom is less widely observed now than in the past, both in Greece and elsewhere.

In the north, the word 'siesta' is not even part of the native vocabulary, and is known in English and German only as a word borrowed from the Spanish. It tends to have slightly negative connotations, carrying overtones of southern sloth, a life of *mañana, mañana*.

Today it is in the dominant northern countries that power and money are concentrated. It is there that important decisions for the future are taken, and the south must simply follow suit.

Northerners tend to be critical of southerners, but their criticisms are those of tourists who resent change. We have all heard it: 'It used to be so beautiful in the south, it was lovely then. Now it's too crowded, there's too much of this ... too much of that ...'. Every year, like migrant birds, tens of millions of fair-skinned people move south in search of the sun, fleeing the disciplined life of the industrialized north. They are always in a hurry, drawn by sunshine and the quality of the southerner's life.

In the south, it is customary to take a short rest, or siesta, after lunch. This quiet time is a source of energy and well-being. More than just an afternoon snooze, a true siesta is a period of waking dreams in which the mind roams freely through the realms of the imagination. A good siesta should be a time of perfect relaxation for both body and mind, without total loss of consciousness. It is not the deep sleep that overcomes us at night: it is a sort of drowsiness to which we succumb, as colours fade, willpower is relinquished and the instincts take over. Time is suspended, the real world melts away, and without conscious effort, a sense of self is restored to the individual.

If you want to learn how to enjoy a good siesta, I recommend that you look to your cat for instruction.

I was born in the north and chose to live in the south, and for me the siesta is very important. During the summer months, having a siesta is as essential as eating or drinking. Without that short period of repose, I simply don't feel at ease with myself.

For cats, it is a sacrosanct time when they must not on any account be disturbed. History tells us that the Prophet Mohammed cut his burnous in two rather than move his cat, which was sleeping peacefully on top of it.

A cat lives according to his desires and moods. He sleeps when he wants, day or night. His forepaws are his pillow, his fur serves as well as any mattress, his tail wraps round his body as though to keep it safe. He dreams a lot, as we see from the way his body twitches and quivers. Sometimes his dreams are so intense that they wake him up.

So-called 'progress' has transformed our perception of time. Everything is happening much more quickly today than it did yesterday, and yet still we run out of time. Speed has become our goal, and yet we are not sure why. We seem to have forgotten that the bits of life we actually remember are the intense experiences, moments that are particularly interesting or pleasant or painful.

12

As the Surrealist poet René Char
says, "The essential is always under threat
from the trivial."

We suffer because of the demands we are
always making on ourselves. In our modern world,
having money has become such a necessity that it seems
impossible to manage without it. That fact imposes terrible
pressures, from which none of us is immune. We no longer
have any time to waste, no time simply to do nothing, to
dream and doze, or in short, to take a siesta.

It is largely for this reason that we so admire our cats.
For modern man, it is a wonderful release to live with
creatures who are free from human stresses and cares.

So, by all means let us admire our feline friends, but let
us also imbibe some of their wisdom and remember that, for them,
life would not be life without the time to enjoy it.